# FOUR-PATCH Frolic

# Barbara Groves And Mary Jacobson

# FOUR-PATCH

## Me and My Sister Designs

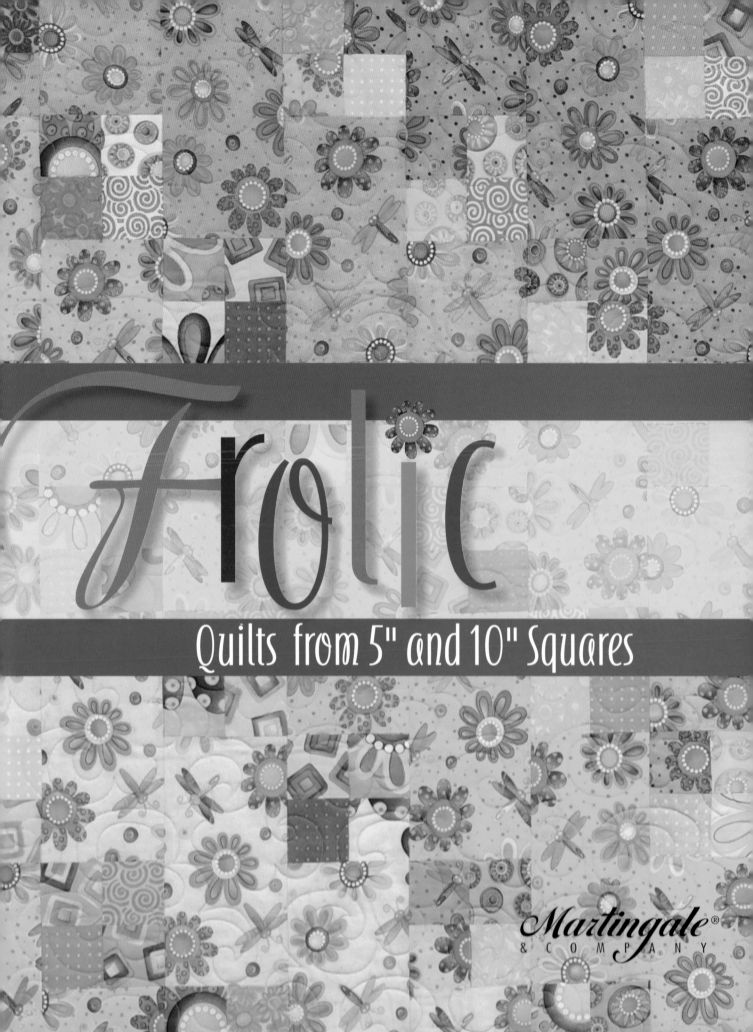

# Frolic

## Quilts from 5" and 10" Squares

*Martingale*® & COMPANY

Four-Patch Frolic:
Quilts from 5" and 10" Squares
© 2009 by Barbara Groves and Mary Jacobson

That Patchwork Place® is an imprint of
Martingale & Company®.

Martingale & Company
20205 144th Ave. NE
Woodinville, WA 98072-8478 USA
www.martingale-pub.com

## CREDITS

President & CEO: Tom Wierzbicki

Editor in Chief: Mary V. Green

Managing Editor: Tina Cook

Developmental Editor: Karen Costello Soltys

Technical Editor: Ellen Pahl

Copy Editor: Marcy Heffernan

Design Director: Stan Green

Production Manager: Regina Girard

Illustrator: Laurel Strand

Cover & Text Designer: Stan Green

Photographer: Brent Kane

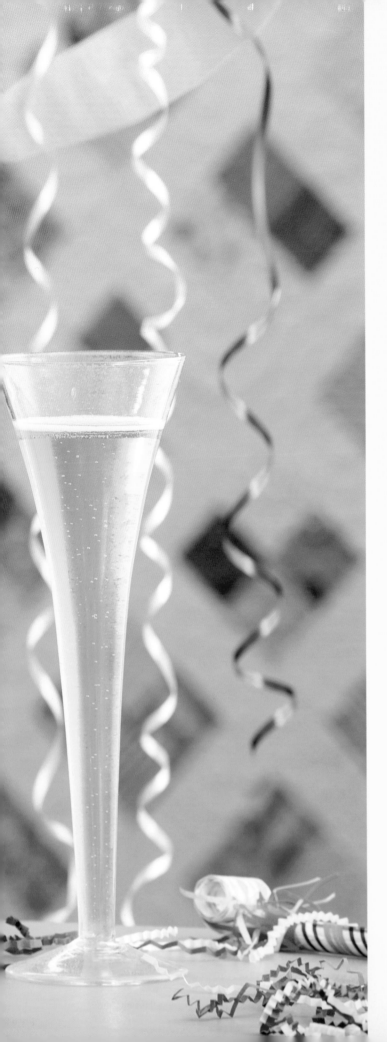

Printed in China

14 13 12 11 10 09          8 7 6 5 4 3 2 1

**Library of Congress Cataloging-in-Publication Data**

Library of Congress Control Number: 2009003174

ISBN: 978-1-56477-903-8

**MISSION STATEMENT**

Dedicated to providing quality products and service to inspire creativity.

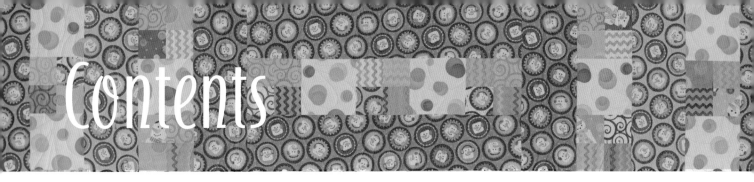

# Contents

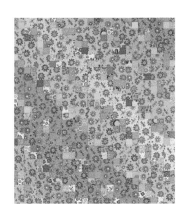

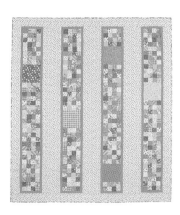

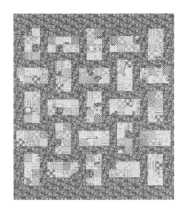

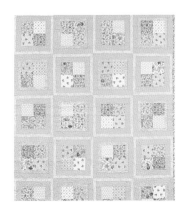

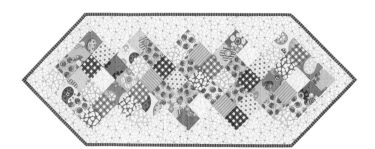

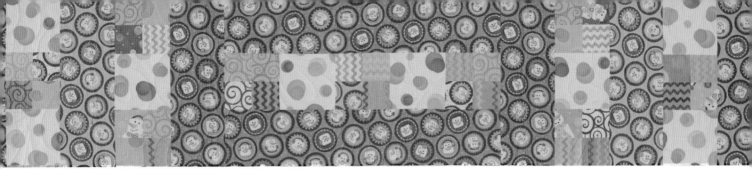

S'MORES •• 38

GEORGE AND
MARTHA •• 42

CONFETTI •• 46

FOUR-PATCH
PILLOWCASE •• 50

BFF •• 54

REBECCA •• 58

SWATCHES •• 64

S-C-H-DOUBLE-OH-L
68

# Introduction

## We always like fast, fun, and easy quilts and are attracted to simple designs.

In that spirit, all of the quilts in this book are based on the classic Four Patch block. It is a favorite—one of those great basic blocks with endless possibilities. While we appreciate all the work that goes into prize-winning quilts, we really love those that are made to be used everyday.

This book is an opportunity for us to showcase some of our recent fabric designs for Moda and to incorporate precut 5" and 10" fabric squares—sometimes referred to as "charms" and "layer cakes," respectively—into our quilts.

We have made many new friends who also design fabrics for Moda, and we've enjoyed using their fabrics throughout this book too. What we like to call "everyday colors"—bright colors that

feel good and bring a smile to your face—are our favorites. The hunt for fabrics to make our quilts never seems to lose its excitement! We are always drawn to the most colorful and whimsical fabrics wherever we shop.

As always, we believe that quilts should be used and loved every day. All of our quilts are pet tested and washer/dryer friendly. Sometimes at our houses there is even a dog or cat cuddling a quilt on a pile of laundry.

We hope you enjoy making some of the fast, fun, and easy quilts in this book and that you and your family will cherish them everyday.

~ *Mary and Barb*

# Aunt Bea

Finished quilt: 50" x 50"  •  Finished block: 8" x 8"

DESIGNED AND PIECED BY BARBARA GROVES AND MARY JACOBSON

Get the chicken frying ...
Barney's coming to dinner!
This easy, nostalgic quilt is
made using the popular
feedsack and 1950s-style
prints. One simple block is all
you will need to create this
fun "down-home" quilt.

## Materials

*All yardages are based on 40"-wide fabric.*

50 coordinating 5" x 5" squares for blocks

1⅞ yards of red print for blocks and border

½ yard of plaid for binding

3¼ yards of fabric for backing

58" x 58" piece of batting

25 white buttons for embellishment

1 skein red DMC floss for tying buttons

## Cutting

From the red print, cut:

13 strips, 2½" x 40"; crosscut into 50
   rectangles, 2½" x 8½"

5 strips, 5¼" x 40"

From the plaid, cut:

6 strips, 2¼" x 40"

## Making the Blocks

**1.** Divide the 50 coordinating 5" squares into 25 pairs of contrasting colors or contrasting values (light and dark).

**2.** Layer each pair of squares right sides together and, using ¼" seam allowance, stitch along two opposite sides of the squares as shown.

**3.** Cut down the center of the squares as shown and press the seam allowances open. Make a total of 50 two-patch units.

Cut.

2½"  2½"

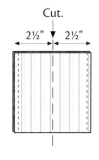  

Make 50.

**4.** Divide the 50 two-patch units from step 3 into 25 *new* combinations of contrasting pairs.

**5.** With right sides together, layer the two-patch units, aligning the seams. Using ¼" seam allowance, stitch along two opposite sides, making sure to stitch across the previous seam lines as shown.

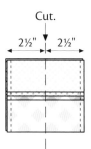

**6.** Cut down the center of the sewn units as shown and press the seam allowances open. Make a total of 50 Four Patch blocks.

Cut.

2½"  2½"

Make 50.

**7.** Arrange and sew two Four Patch blocks and two red print 2½" x 8½" rectangles into blocks as shown. The blocks should now measure 8½" x 8½" square. Make a total of 25 blocks.

Make 25.

## Assembling the Quilt

**1.** Arrange the blocks into five rows of five blocks each, alternating the direction of the blocks as shown.

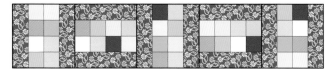

Make 3.

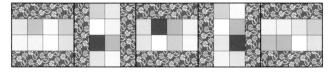

Make 2.

**2.** Sew the rows together, referring to the quilt assembly diagram on page 13. The quilt should now measure 40½" x 40½".

## Adding the Border

**1.** Piece five red print 5¼" x 40" border strips together, end to end.

**2.** Measure the quilt from top to bottom through the middle to determine the length of the side borders. From the pieced strip, cut side borders to the needed length and attach them to the sides of the quilt.

**3.** Measure the quilt from side to side through the middle, including the side borders, to determine the length of the top and bottom borders. From the pieced strip, cut the top and bottom borders to the needed length and attach them to the top and bottom of the quilt.

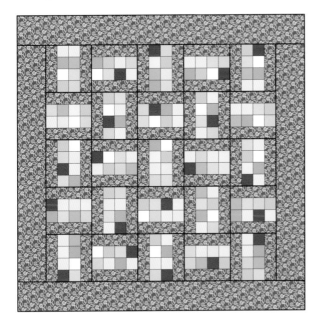

## Finishing

**1.** Refer to "Finishing" on page 75 to layer, baste, quilt, and add binding using the plaid 2½" x 40" strips.

**2.** Decorate the quilt with your favorite buttons and tie them on using a needle and embroidery floss.

# Easy Pincushion

Finished pincushion: 4" x 4"

DESIGNED AND PIECED BY BARBARA GROVES AND MARY JACOBSON

Aunt Bea's sewing basket wouldn't be complete without this easy-to-make pincushion. All her pins and needles are where they belong and ready to use whenever Andy's uniform needs a quick repair or a button sewn back on. She's made them for all the ladies in her sewing circle.

## Materials

4 coordinating squares, 2½" x 2½" for Four Patch★

1 square, 4½" x 4½", for pincushion back

3 buttons for embellishment

10" length of 6-ply embroidery floss for tying buttons

½ cup poly pellets for stuffing

★Or 1 leftover Four Patch block, 4½" x 4½" unfinished

## Making the Pincushion

**1.** Sew the four 2½" squares together as shown to make the Four Patch block for the pincushion top.

**2.** Layer the Four Patch block and the backing square right sides together. Stitch around all four sides of the layered squares, leaving a 1" to 2" opening for stuffing along one side. Backstitch at the beginning and end of the stitching.

**3.** Turn the pincushion right side out and press the seam allowances at the opening to the inside.

**4.** Fill with poly pellets. Do not overfill!

**5.** Hand stitch the opening closed.

## Finishing

**1.** Stack and center two buttons on the top and center one button on the bottom of the pincushion. Thread a needle with the 6-ply strand of embroidery floss. Beginning on the top, insert the needle through one hole of both the top two buttons, take it through the pincushion and through one hole of the bottom button.

**2.** Insert the needle through the second hole of the bottom button and back to the top through the second hole of the top buttons.

**3.** Tie the two ends of the embroidery floss, pulling the thread taut to draw the front and back buttons together. Clip the ends of the floss.

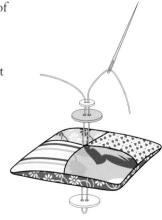

# Tangerine Tango

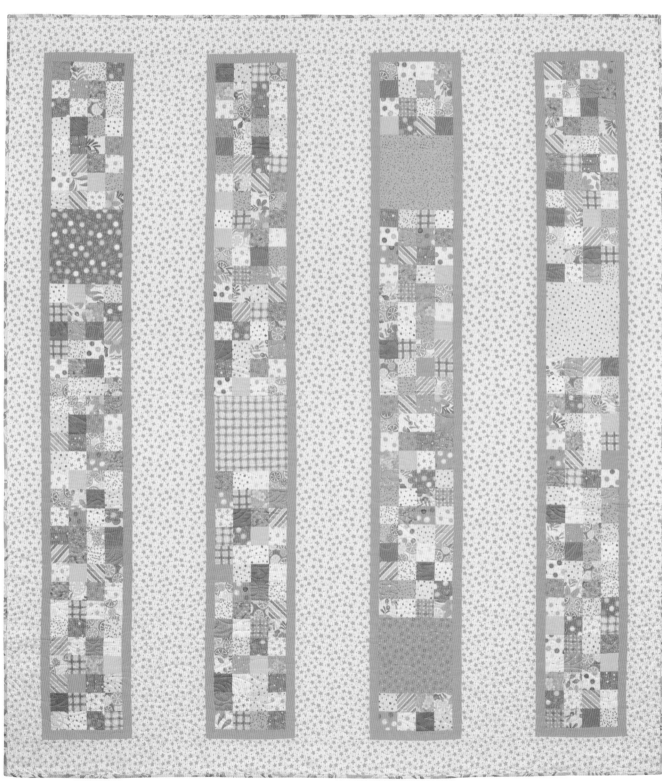

Finished quilt: 72" x 82"  •  Finished block: 4" x 8"

DESIGNED AND PIECED BY BARBARA GROVES AND MARY JACOBSON

When we first started designing this quilt, it looked nothing like it does now. Twice a year we go to Quilt Camp with our friends, and we brought this quilt along to work on. After numerous helpful comments from the peanut gallery, things got switched around, and even the original name was changed! Thanks, Deb!

## Materials

*All yardages are based on 40"-wide fabric*

124 coordinating 5" x 5" squares for blocks

5 coordinating 10" x 10" squares for blocks

2⅞ yards of cream-and-orange print for sashing and border

⅞ yard of orange solid for row borders

⅔ yard of green print for binding

5½ yards of fabric for backing

80" x 90" piece of batting

## Cutting

From the 10" squares, cut:

5 squares, 8½" x 8½"

From the orange solid, cut:

3 strips, 1½" x 40"; crosscut into 8 rectangles, 1½" x 10½"

15 strips, 1½" x 40"

From the cream-and-orange print, cut:

3 strips, 8½" x 74½", from the *lengthwise* grain, for sashing

2 strips, 4¼" x 74½", from the *lengthwise* grain, for side borders

4 strips, 4¼" x 40", from the *crosswise* grain, for top and bottom borders

From the green print, cut:

8 strips, 2¼" x 40"

**4.** Divide the 124 two-patch units from step 3 into 62 *new* combinations of contrasting pairs.

**5.** With right sides together, layer the two-patch units, aligning the seams. Using ¼" seam allowance, stitch along two opposite sides, making sure to stitch across the previous seam lines as shown.

**6.** Cut down the center of the sewn units as shown and press the seam allowances open. Make a total of 124 Four Patch blocks.

Cut.

2½"   2½"

Make 124.

**7.** Arrange and sew two Four Patch blocks together as shown. The Eight Patch blocks should now measure 4½" x 8½". Make a total of 62 blocks.

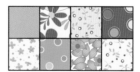

Make 62.

## Making the Blocks

**1.** Divide the 124 coordinating 5" squares into 62 pairs, combining two contrasting colors or contrasting values (light and dark).

**2.** Layer each pair of squares right sides together and, using ¼" seam allowance, stitch along two opposite sides of the squares as shown.

**3.** Cut down the center of the squares as shown and press the seam allowances open. Make a total of 124 two-patch units.

Cut.

2½"   2½"

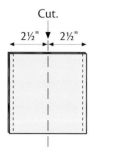  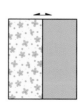

Make 124.

## Assembling the Rows

Arrange and sew the blocks into rows as follows:

**Row 1:** 16 blocks and one 8½" square.

**Row 2:** 16 blocks and one 8½" square.

**Row 3:** 14 blocks and two 8½" squares.

**Row 4:** 16 blocks and one 8½" square.

The vertical rows should all measure 8½" x 72½".

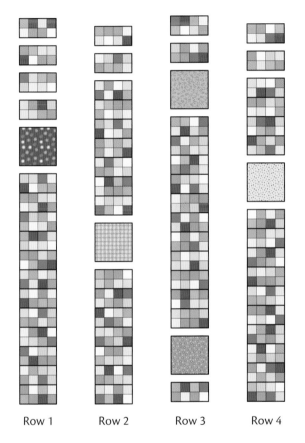

Row 1    Row 2    Row 3    Row 4

## Adding Borders and Sashing

**1.** Piece the 15 orange 1½" x 40" strips together end to end. From this pieced strip, cut 8 strips, 1½" x 72½".

**2.** Attach 1½" x 72½" strips to both sides of each vertical row and orange 1½" x 10½" rectangles to the top and bottom of each row. Press all seam allowances toward the orange strips. The rows should now measure 10½" x 74½".

**3.** Beginning with row 1, sew a cream-and-orange 8½" x 74½" sashing strip between each vertical row as shown in the quilt diagram. Press seam allowances toward the sashing. The quilt center should now measure 64½" x 74½".

**4.** Attach a cream-and-orange 4¼" x 74½" border strip to each side of the quilt. Press the seam allowances toward the cream and orange borders.

**5.** Piece four cream-and-orange 4¼" x 40" border strips together end to end. From this pieced strip, cut two strips, 4¼" x 72"; press.

**6.** Attach 4¼" x 72" border strips to the top and bottom of the quilt; press.

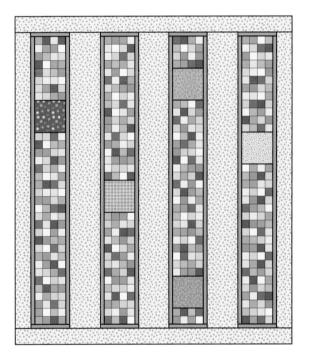

## Finishing

Refer to "Finishing" on page 75 to layer, baste, quilt, and add binding using the green print 2¼" x 40" strips.

# Gum Chain

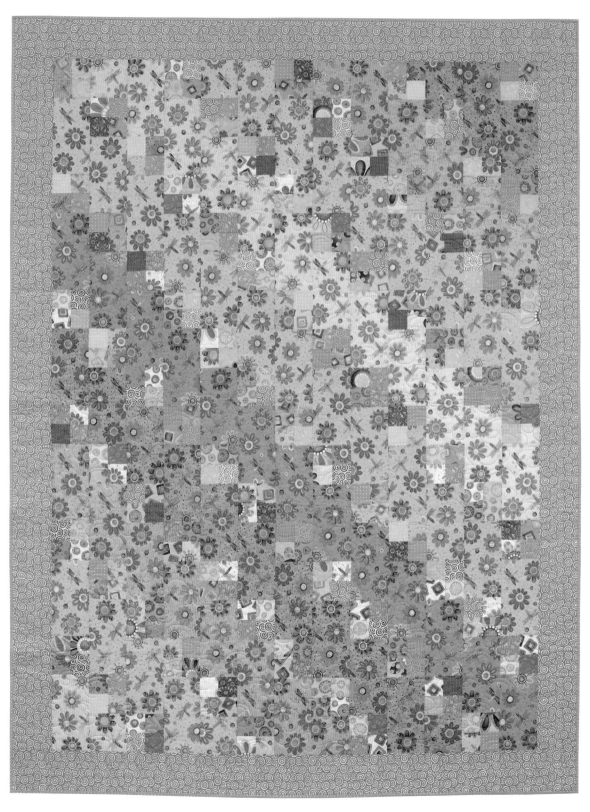

Finished quilt: 61" x 81"  •  Finished block: 4" x 4"

DESIGNED AND PIECED BY MARY JACOBSON AND BARBARA GROVES

Did you know that the world's longest gum-wrapper chain is 52,913 feet long and contains 1,240,000 gum wrappers? Do you remember Beeman's, Blackjack, Adam's Sour, Clark's Cinnamon, and Fruit Stripe gum? Making gum chains was one of our favorite summertime crafts as children, and for some reason this quilt reminds us of those chains.

## Materials

*All yardages are based on 40"-wide fabric.*

78 coordinating 5" x 5" squares for blocks

⅝ yard *each* of yellow, orange, pink, purple, turquoise, and green prints for blocks

1¼ yards of turquoise print for border

⅝ yard of turquoise print for binding

5¼ yards of fabric for backing

69" x 89" piece of batting

## Cutting

From the yellow print, cut:
4 strips, 4½" x 40"; crosscut into:
    12 rectangles, 4½" x 8½"
    2 squares, 4½" x 4½"

From the orange print, cut:
4 strips, 4½" x 40"; crosscut into:
    12 rectangles, 4½" x 8½"
    2 squares, 4½" x 4½"

From the pink print, cut:
4 strips, 4½" x 40"; crosscut into:
    12 rectangles, 4½" x 8½"
    2 squares, 4½" x 4½"

From the purple print, cut:
4 strips, 4½" x 40"; crosscut into:
    12 rectangles, 4½" x 8½"
    2 squares, 4½" x 4½"

From the turquoise print for blocks, cut:
4 strips, 4½" x 40"; crosscut into 13 rectangles, 4½" x 8½"

From the green print, cut:
4 strips, 4½" x 40"; crosscut into 13 rectangles, 4½" x 8½"

From the turquoise print for border, cut:
8 strips, 4¾" x 40"

From the turquoise print for binding, cut:
8 strips, 2¼" x 40"

## Making the Blocks

**1.** Divide the 78 coordinating 5" squares into 39 pairs of contrasting colors or contrasting values (light and dark).

**2.** Layer each pair of squares right sides together and, using a ¼" seam allowance, stitch along two opposite sides of the squares as shown.

**3.** Cut down the center of the squares as shown and press the seam allowances open. Make a total of 78 two-patch units.

Cut.

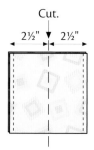  

Make 78.

**4.** Divide the 78 two-patch units from step 3 into 39 *new* combinations of contrasting pairs.

**5.** With right sides together, layer the two-patch units, aligning the seams. Using ¼" seam allowance, stitch along two opposite sides, making sure to stitch across the previous seam lines as shown.

**6.** Cut down the center of the sewn units as shown and press the seam allowances open. Make a total of 78 Four Patch blocks. The blocks should measure 4½" x 4½".

Cut.

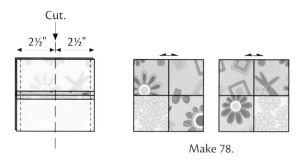

Make 78.

## Assembling the Quilt

**1.** Referring to the assembly diagram, arrange and sew the Four Patch blocks, rectangles, and squares into 13 vertical rows as shown. Sew the rows together. The quilt center should now measure 52½" x 72½".

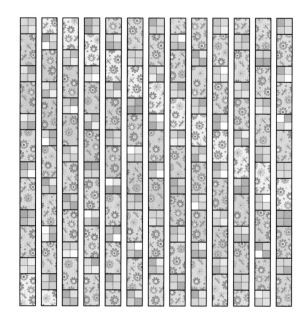

**2.** Piece the eight turquoise 4¾" x 40" border strips together end to end.

**3.** Measure the quilt from top to bottom through the middle to determine the length of the side borders. From the pieced strip, cut the side borders to the needed length and attach them to the sides of the quilt.

**4.** Measure the quilt from side to side through the middle including the side borders to determine the length of the top and bottom borders. From the pieced strip, cut the top and bottom borders to the needed length and attach them to the top and bottom of the quilt.

## Finishing

Refer to Finishing on page 75 to layer, baste, quilt, and add the binding using the turquoise print 2¼" x 40" strips.

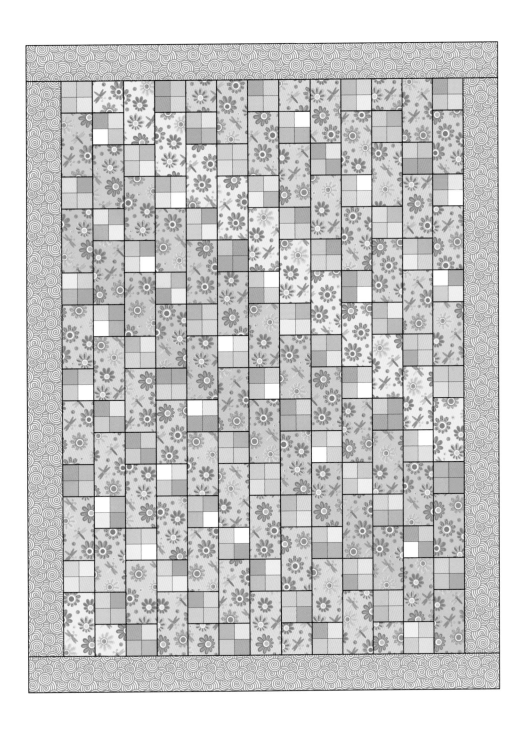

# Brimfield

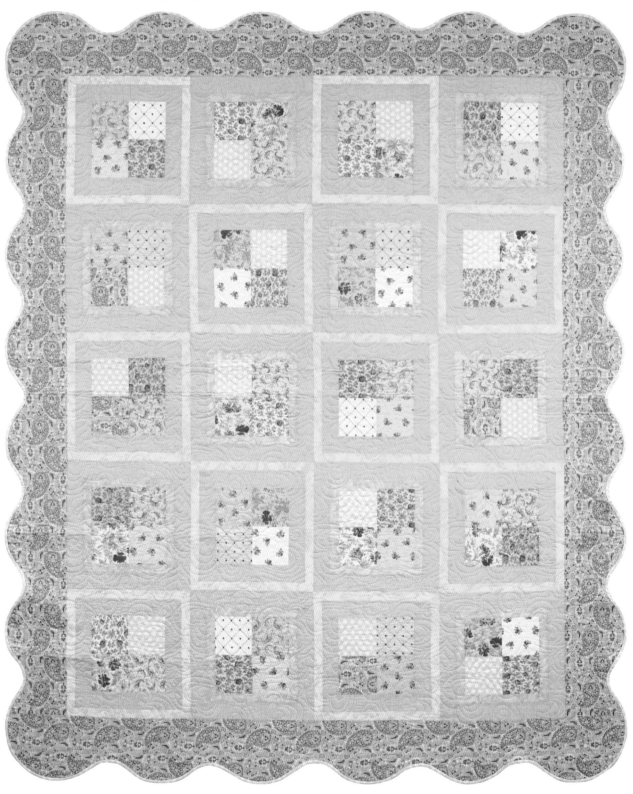

Finished quilt: 76" x 91"  •  Finished block: 15" x 15"

DESIGNED AND PIECED BY BARBARA GROVES AND MARY JACOBSON

After a business trip to Sturbridge, Massachusetts, we had an extra day and a rental car that we couldn't let go to waste! So, we drove down the road to a small town named Brimfield. We visited some wonderful antique stores. Besides finding a great cranberry glass sugar shaker, we found a beautiful old serving platter that inspired this quilt.

## Materials

*All yardages are based on 40"-wide fabric.*

20 coordinating 10" x 10" squares for blocks
2½ yards of pink striped fabric for blocks
2 yards of pink floral for border
1 yard of yellow print for blocks
⅝ yard of blue print for blocks
1 yard of green print for bias binding
8½ yards of fabric for backing
84" x 99" piece of batting

## Cutting

From the yellow print, cut:
20 strips, 1½" x 40"; crosscut into:
    20 rectangles, 1½" x 13½"
    20 rectangles, 1½" x 15½"

From the blue print, cut:
12 strips, 1½" x 40"; crosscut into:
    20 rectangles, 1½" x 9½"
    20 rectangles, 1½" x 11½"

From the pink striped fabric, cut:
32 strips, 2½" x 40"; crosscut into:
    20 rectangles, 2½" x 9½"
    20 rectangles, 2½" x 11½"
    20 rectangles, 2½" x 13½"
    20 rectangles, 2½" x 15½"

From the pink floral, cut:
8 strips, 8¼" x 40"

From the green print, cut:
1 square, 35" x 35"

## Making the Blocks

**1.** Divide the 20 coordinating 10" squares into 10 pairs of contrasting colors or contrasting values (light and dark).

**2.** Layer each pair of squares right sides together and, using ¼" seam allowance, stitch along two opposite sides of the squares as shown.

**3.** Cut down the center of the squares as shown and the press the seam allowances open. Make a total of 20 two-patch units.

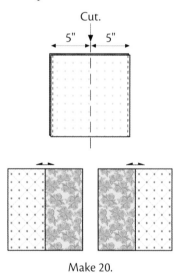

Cut.

5" | 5"

Make 20.

**4.** Divide the 20 two-patch units from step 3 into 10 *new* combinations of contrasting pairs.

**5.** With right sides together, layer the two-patch units, aligning the seams. Using ¼" seam allowance, stitch along two opposite sides, making sure to stitch across the previous seam lines as shown.

**6.** Cut down the center of the sewn units as shown and press the seam allowances open. Make a total of 20 Four Patch blocks.

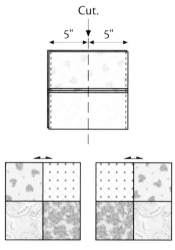

Cut.

5" | 5"

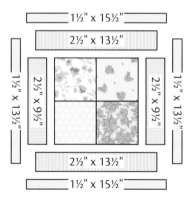

Make 20.

**7.** Arrange one Four Patch block, two pink striped 2½" x 9½" rectangles, two pink striped 2½" x 13½" rectangles, two yellow 1½" x 13½" rectangles, and two yellow 1½" x 15½" rectangles as shown. Sew them together to make a block. Make 10 yellow blocks. The blocks should measure 15½" x 15½".

1½" x 15½"
2½" x 13½"
1½" x 13½" | 2½" x 9½" | 2½" x 9½" | 1½" x 13½"
2½" x 13½"
1½" x 15½"

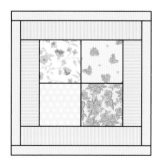

Make 10.

**8.** Arrange one Four Patch block, two blue 1½" x 9½" rectangles, two blue 1½" x 11½" rectangles, two pink striped 2½" x 11½" rectangles, and two pink striped 2½" x 15½" rectangles as shown. Sew them together to make a block. Make 10 pink blocks. The blocks should measure 15½" x 15½".

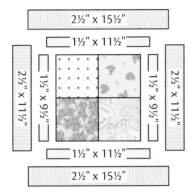

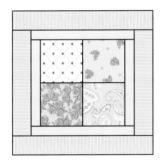

Make 10.

## Assembling the Quilt

**1.** Sew the blocks into five rows of four blocks each, alternating the blocks as shown.

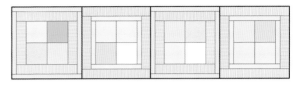

Make 3.

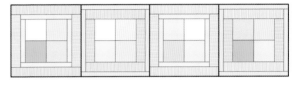

Make 2.

**2.** Referring to the quilt diagram on page 28, arrange and sew the rows together. The quilt should now measure 60½" x 75½".

## Adding the Border

**1.** Piece the eight pink floral 8¼" x 40" border strips together end to end.

**2.** Measure the quilt from top to bottom through the middle to determine the length of the side borders. From the pieced strip, cut the side borders to the needed length and attach them to the sides of the quilt.

**3.** Measure the quilt from side to side through the middle, including the side borders, to determine the length of the top and bottom borders. From the pieced strip, cut the top and bottom borders to the needed length and attach them to the top and bottom of the quilt.

## Finishing

Refer to Finishing on page 75 to layer, baste, and quilt as desired. Trim the edges of the quilt with the scallop pattern on page 29 and add green print bias binding, referring to page 77.

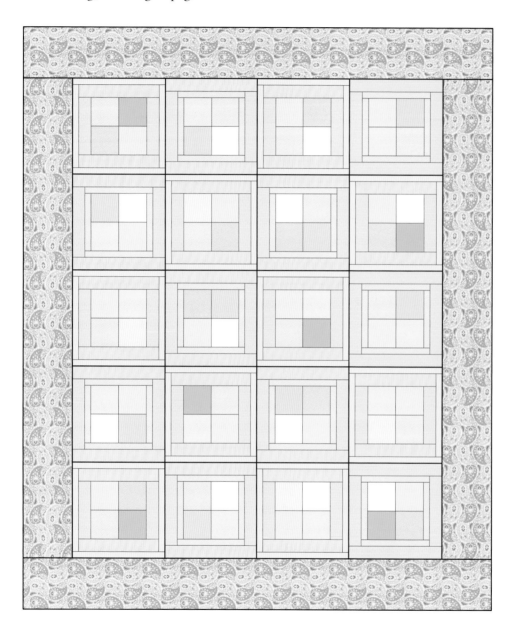

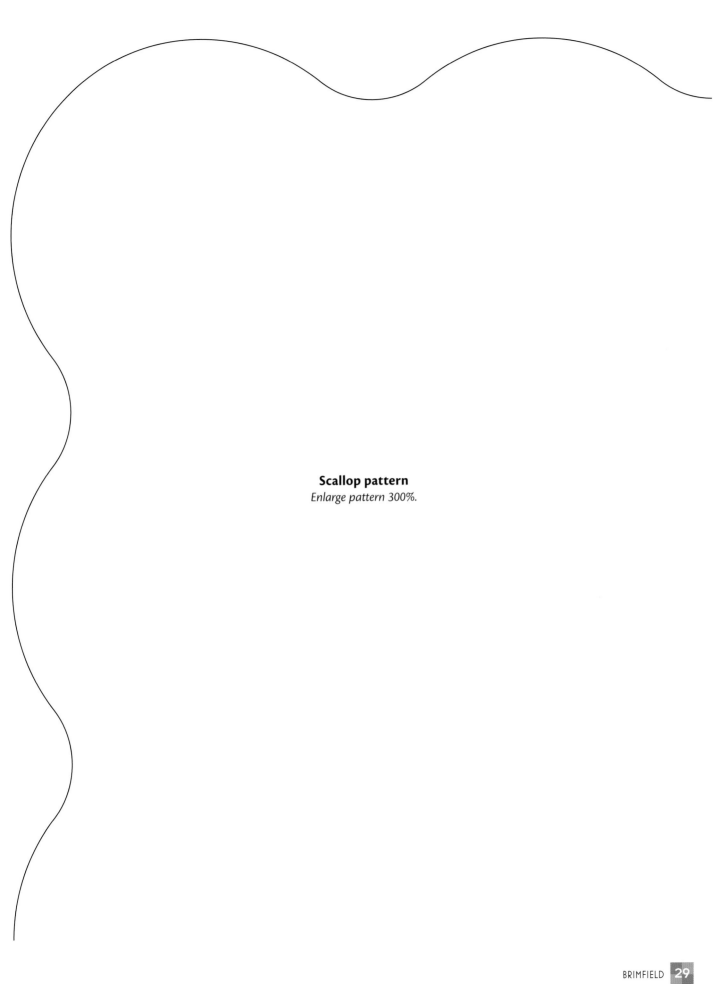

**Scallop pattern**
*Enlarge pattern 300%.*

# Berries in a Box

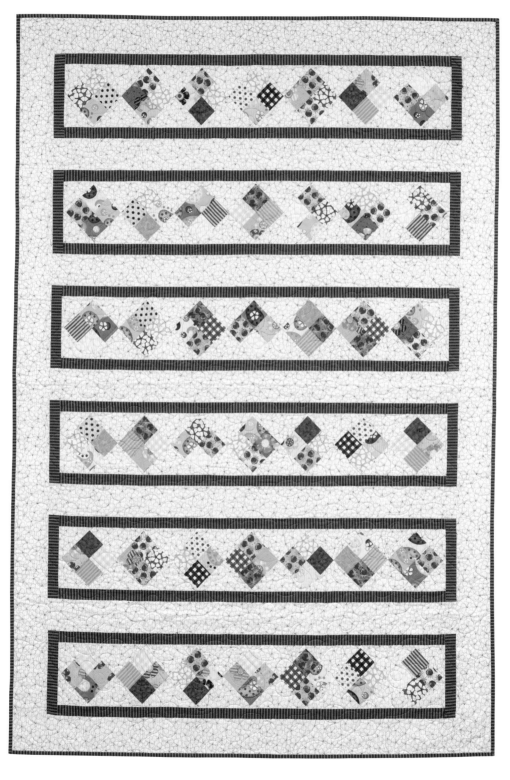

Finished quilt: 48½" x 69½"  •  Finished block: 4" x 4"

DESIGNED AND PIECED BY MARY JACOBSON AND BARBARA GROVES

Whether you are making shortcake or this quilt, collecting berries is lots of fun! We used one of our favorite fabric collections in this refreshing summertime quilt. Quilts with berries will always be in season!

## Materials

*All yardages are based on 40"-wide fabric.*

42 coordinating 5" x 5" squares for blocks

3 yards of light print for setting triangles, sashing, and border

1⅓ yards of blue striped fabric for row borders and binding

4½ yards of fabric for backing

54½" x 77½" piece of batting

## Cutting

**From the light print, cut:**

5 strips, 8½" x 40"; crosscut into 18 squares, 8½" x 8½". Cut each square twice diagonally to yield 72 side setting triangles.★

2 strips, 5½" x 40"; crosscut into 12 squares, 5½" x 5½". Cut each square once diagonally to yield 24 corner setting triangles.★

12 strips, 3½" x 40"

**From the blue striped fabric, cut:**

3 strips, 1½" x 40"; crosscut into 12 rectangles, 1½" x 8½"

12 strips, 1½" x 40½"★★

7 strips, 2¼" x 40"

★*Side and corner setting triangles are cut larger than needed and will extend beyond blocks.*

★★*If your fabric is not wide enough, cut 13 strips and piece them together before cutting.*

## Making the Blocks

**1.** Divide the 42 coordinating 5" squares into 21 pairs, combining two contrasting colors or contrasting values (light and dark).

**2.** Layer each pair of squares right sides together and, using ¼" seam allowance, stitch along two opposite sides of the squares as shown.

**3.** Cut down the center of the squares as shown and press the seam allowances open. Make a total of 42 two-patch units.

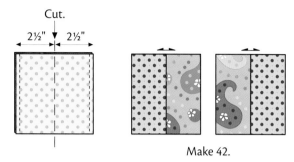

Make 42.

**4.** Divide the 42 two-patch units from step 3 into 21 *new* combinations of contrasting pairs.

**5.** With right sides together, layer the two-patch units, aligning the seams. Using ¼" seam allowance, stitch along two opposite sides, making sure to stitch across the previous seam lines as shown.

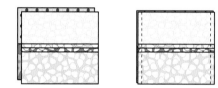

**6.** Cut down the center of the sewn units as shown and press the seam allowances open. Make a total of 42 Four Patch blocks. The blocks should measure 4½" x 4½".

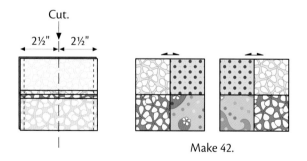

Make 42.

## Assembling the Rows

**1.** Arrange seven Four Patch blocks, 12 side setting triangles, and four corner setting triangles in a row and sew the pieces together in diagonal sections as shown. Trim the excess from the triangle points and join the diagonal sections. Crease the corner triangles in the center, align the creases with the center seam of the Four Patch blocks, and attach the corner triangles.

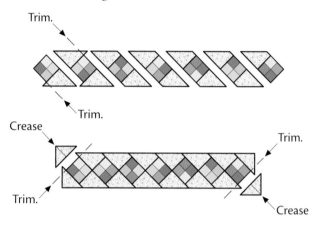

**2.** Trim the row to measure 6½" x 40½". Make a total of six rows.

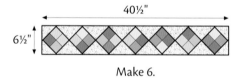

Make 6.

**3.** Attach blue striped 1½" x 40½" row border strips to the top and bottom of each row. Press toward the blue striped fabric. Attach blue striped 1½" x 8½" rectangles to the end of each row and press toward the blue striped fabric. Each row should now measure 8½" x 42½".

## Assembling the Quilt

**1.** Piece six light print 3½" x 40" strips together end to end for the sashing. From the pieced strip, cut five sashing strips, 3½" x 42½".

**2.** Referring to the quilt diagram, arrange and sew a sashing strip between each row. The quilt should now measure 42½" x 63½".

**3.** Piece six light print 3½" x 40" strips together end to end for the borders.

**4.** Measure the quilt from top to bottom through the middle to determine the length of the side borders. From the pieced strip, cut side borders to the needed length and attach them to the sides of the quilt. Press toward the borders.

**5.** Measure the quilt from side to side through the middle including the side borders to determine the length of the top and bottom borders. From the pieced strip, cut the top and bottom borders to the needed length and attach them to the quilt; press.

## Finishing

Refer to "Finishing" on page 75 to layer, baste, quilt, and add the binding using the blue striped 2¼" x 40" strips.

Quilt assembly

# Berry Easy Table Topper

Finished quilt: 15" x 39"  •  Finished block: 4" x 4"

DESIGNED AND PIECED BY MARY JACOBSON AND BARBARA GROVES

This quick and easy table topper is a must for any picnic table! Bright, cheerful, and fast, it will be done long before the baked beans and potato salad are ready. On second thought, maybe not that fast, but still faster than getting the kids to set the table!

## Materials

*All yardages are based on 40"-wide fabric.*

16 coordinating 5" x 5" squares for blocks

½ yard of light print for setting triangles and setting rectangles

¼ yard of blue striped fabric for binding

1½ yards of fabric for backing

23" x 47" piece of batting

## Cutting

From the light print, cut:

1 strip, 10" x 40"; crosscut into 2 squares, 10" x 10". Cut each square twice diagonally to yield 8 setting triangles.

2 strips, 2" x 40"; crosscut into:

    2 rectangles, 2" x 12"

    2 rectangles, 2" x 14"

From the blue striped fabric, cut:

3 strips, 2¼" x 40"

## Making the Blocks

**1.** Divide the 16 coordinating 5" squares into eight pairs of contrasting colors or contrasting values (light and dark).

**2.** Layer the pairs of squares right sides together and, using ¼" seam allowance, stitch along two opposite sides of the squares as shown.

**3.** Cut down the center of the squares as shown and press the seam allowances open. Make a total of 16 two-patch units.

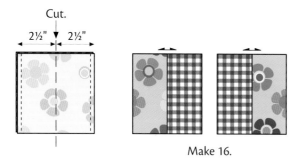

Cut.

2½"  2½"

Make 16.

**4.** Divide the 16 two-patch units from step 3 into 8 *new* combinations of contrasting pairs.

**5.** With right sides together, layer the two-patch units, aligning the seams. Using a ¼" seam allowance, stitch along two opposite sides, making sure to stitch across the previous seam lines as shown.

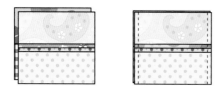

**6.** Cut down the center of the sewn units as shown and press the seam allowances open. The blocks should now measure 4½" x 4½". Make 16 blocks.

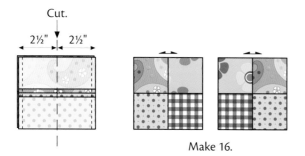

Cut.

2½"  2½"

Make 16.

## Assembling the Quilt

**1.** Arrange and sew the Four Patch blocks and setting triangles together in diagonal rows. Trim the excess from the points of the triangles. Sew the rows together.

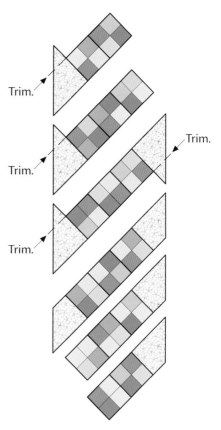

Trim.

Trim.

Trim.

Trim.

Trim.

**2.** Trim any remaining triangle points as needed and add the 2" x 12" and then the 2" x 14" rectangles as shown. Press the seam allowances toward the rectangles and trim the table topper to measure 15" wide.

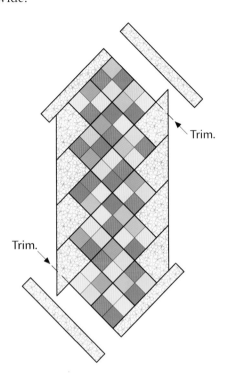

Trim.

Trim.

## Finishing

Refer to "Finishing" on page 75 to layer, baste, quilt, and add binding using the blue striped 2¼" x 40" strips. Refer to "Mitering 135° Corners" on page 76 when adding the binding.

# S'mores

Finished quilt: 60½" x 76½" • Finished block: 4" x 4"

DESIGNED AND PIECED BY MARY JACOBSON AND BARBARA GROVES

What's more fun than rows of marshmallow snowmen, chocolate, and graham crackers! Get warm and toasty and have fun making a no-calorie version of this gooey favorite.

## Materials

*All yardages are based on 40"-wide fabric.*

64 coordinating 5" x 5" squares for blocks

1⅛ yards of white polka-dot fabric for blocks

1 yard of pink print for border 4

¾ yard of turquoise print for border 3

⅝ yard of green print for border 2

⅓ yard of purple print for border 1

⅝ yard of pink print for binding

5¼ yards of fabric for backing

69" x 85" piece of batting

## Cutting

From the white polka-dot fabric, cut:

8 strips, 4½" x 40"; crosscut into 62 squares, 4½" x 4½"

From the purple print for border 1, cut:

2 strips, 4½" x 40"; crosscut into:

    2 rectangles, 4½" x 12½"

    2 rectangles, 4½" x 20½"

From the green print for border 2, cut:

4 strips, 4½" x 40"; crosscut into:

    2 strips, 4½" x 36½"

    2 strips, 4½" x 28½"

From the turquoise print for border 3, cut:

5 strips, 4½" x 40"

From the pink print for border 4, cut:

7 strips, 4½" x 40"

From the pink print for binding, cut:

8 strips, 2¼" x 40"

## Making the Blocks

**1.** Divide the 64 coordinating 5" squares into 32 pairs of contrasting colors or contrasting values (light and dark).

**2.** Layer each pair of squares right sides together and, using ¼" seam allowance, stitch along two opposite sides of the squares as shown.

**3.** Cut down the center of the squares as shown and press the seam allowances open. Make a total of 64 two-patch units.

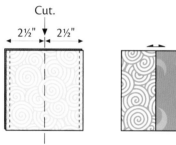

Make 64.

**4.** Divide the 64 two-patch units from step 3 into 32 *new* combinations of contrasting pairs.

**5.** With right sides together, layer the two-patch units, aligning the seams. Using ¼" seam allowance, stitch along two opposite sides, making sure to stitch across the previous seam lines as shown.

**6.** Cut down the center of the sewn units as shown and press the seam allowances open. Make a total of 64 Four Patch blocks. You will use 63; one will be extra. The blocks should measure 4½" x 4½".

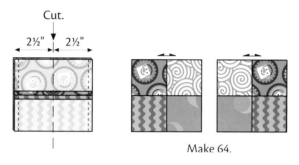

Make 64.

## Assembling the Quilt

Refer to the quilt diagram throughout these steps. Press all seam allowances in the block rows toward the unpieced squares; press all the other seam allowances toward the borders as they are added. You will build the quilt outward from the center.

**1.** Arrange three Four Patch blocks and two white polka-dot 4½" squares and sew them into a vertical row as shown to form the quilt center.

**2.** Sew a purple 4½" x 20½" rectangle to each side of the unit from step 1 and a purple 4½" x 12½" rectangle to the top and bottom as shown.

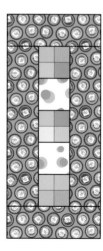

**3.** Arrange and sew four Four Patch blocks and three white polka-dot 4½" squares into a vertical row. Make two rows and attach them to the sides of the unit from step 2.

**4.** Arrange and sew three white polka-dot 4½" squares and two Four Patch blocks into a horizontal row. Make two rows and attach them to the top and bottom of the unit from step 3.

**5.** Sew green 4½" x 36½" border strips to each side of the unit from step 4 and green 4½" x 28½" border strips to the top and bottom.

**6.** Arrange and sew six white polka-dot 4½" squares and five Four Patch blocks into a vertical row. Make two rows and attach them to the sides of the unit from step 5.

**7.** Arrange and sew five Four Patch blocks and four white polka-dot 4½" squares into a horizontal row. Make two rows and attach them to the top and bottom of the unit from step 6.

**8.** Piece together five turquoise 4½" x 40" border strips end to end. From this strip, cut two 52½" side borders and two 44½" top and bottom borders.

**9.** Sew turquoise 4½" x 52½" borders to each side of the unit from step 7 and turquoise 4½" x 44½" borders to the top and bottom.

**10.** Arrange and sew eight Four Patch blocks and seven white polka-dot 4½" squares into a vertical row. Make two rows and attach them to the sides of the unit from step 9.

**11.** Arrange and sew seven white polka-dot 4½" squares and six Four Patch blocks into a horizontal row. Make two rows and attach them to the top and bottom of the unit from step 10.

**12.** Piece together seven pink 4½" x 40" border strips end to end. From this pieced strip, cut two 68½" side borders and two 60½" top and bottom borders.

**13.** Sew pink 4½" x 68½" borders to each side of the quilt and pink 4½" x 60½" borders to the top and bottom of the quilt. The quilt should now measure 60½" x 76½".

## Finishing

Refer to "Finishing" on page 75 to layer, baste, quilt, and add the binding using the pink print 2¼" x 40" strips.

# George and Martha

Finished quilt: 80" x 80" • Finished blocks: 9" x 9"

DESIGNED AND PIECED BY MARY JACOBSON AND BARBARA GROVES

These fabrics go together like George and Martha! The project in one of our very first quilt classes was a patriotic flag quilt. We got in trouble for pressing our seam allowances open—but we didn't care then, and we still don't. Some would say we march to a different drummer! This quilt is red, white, blue, and easy!

## Materials

*All yardages are based on 40"-wide fabric.*

3¾ yards of blue floral for blocks, border, and binding

1⅛ yards of red print for Rail blocks

⅔ yard of light blue print for Four Patch blocks

⅔ yard of dark blue print for Four Patch blocks

½ yard of light paisley print for Rail blocks

½ yard of medium blue print for Rail blocks

½ yard of light blue striped fabric for Rail blocks

7½ yards of fabric for backing

88" x 88" piece of batting

## Cutting

From the light blue print, cut:
2 strips, 10" x 40"; crosscut into 8 squares, 10" x 10"

From the dark blue print, cut:
2 strips, 10" x 40"; crosscut into 8 squares, 10" x 10"

From the light paisley, cut:
6 strips, 2" x 40"

From the medium blue print, cut:
6 strips, 2" x 40"

From the light blue striped fabric, cut:
6 strips, 2" x 40"

From the red print, cut:
12 strips, 2¾" x 40"

From the blue floral, cut:
3 strips, 9½" x 40"; crosscut into 9 squares, 9½" x 9½"

8 strips, 8¾" x 40"

9 strips, 2¼" x 40"

## Making the Four Patch Blocks

**1.** Layer one light blue 10" square and one dark blue 10" square right sides together. Using ¼" seam allowance, stitch along two opposite sides of the squares as shown. Make eight.

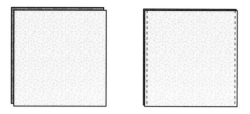

**2.** Cut down the center of the squares as shown and press the seam allowances open. Make a total of 16 two-patch units.

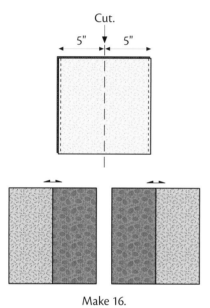

Make 16.

**3.** With right sides together, layer the two-patch units, aligning the seams and reversing the color placement as shown. Using ¼" seam allowance, stitch along two opposite sides, making sure to stitch across the previous seam lines.

**4.** Cut down the center of the sewn units as shown and press the seam allowances open. Make a total of 16 Four Patch blocks. The blocks should measure 9½" x 9½".

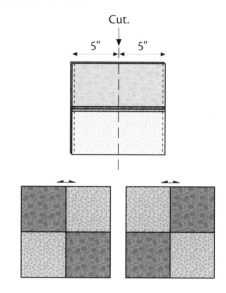

## Making the Rail Blocks

Make a strip set by sewing a light paisley 2 " x 40" strip to one side of a medium blue 2" x 40" strip and a light blue striped 2" x 40" strip to the other side. Add a red 2¾" x 40" strip to each side. Make six strip sets and crosscut them into 24 segments measuring 9½" x 9½".

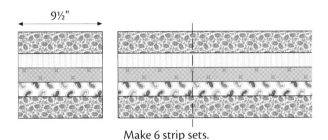

9½"

Make 6 strip sets.
Cut 24 segments.

## Assembling the Quilt

**I.** Alternating the blocks and blue floral squares, arrange and sew seven rows of seven blocks each as shown. Make sure that the Four Patch and Rail blocks are positioned correctly.

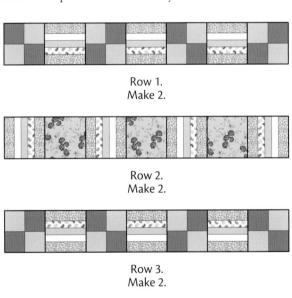

Row 1.
Make 2.

Row 2.
Make 2.

Row 3.
Make 2.

Row 4.
Make 1.

**2.** Referring to the quilt diagram, arrange and sew the rows as shown. The quilt should now measure 63½" x 63½".

**3.** Piece eight blue floral 8¾" x 40" border strips together end to end.

**4.** Measure the quilt from top to bottom through the middle to determine the length of the side borders. From the pieced strip, cut the side borders to the needed length and attach them to the sides of the quilt.

**5.** Measure the quilt from side to side through the middle including the side borders to determine the length of the top and bottom borders. From the pieced strip, cut the top and bottom borders to the needed length and attach them to the quilt.

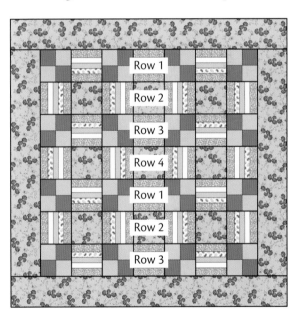

## Finishing

Refer to "Finishing" on page 75 to layer, baste, quilt, and add the binding using the blue floral 2¼" x 40" strips.

# Confetti

Finished quilt: 60½" x 69"  •  Finished block: 4" x 4"

DESIGNED AND PIECED BY MARY JACOBSON AND BARBARA GROVES

This quilt really did start with Four Patch blocks–lots of them! Because we were using our favorite bright colors, we found it hard to stop sewing. Once we placed the Four Patch blocks on point with a crisp white background, we both screamed, "Confetti!"

## Materials

*All yardages are based on 40"-wide fabric.*

98 coordinating 5" x 5" squares for blocks

3¾ yards of white solid for sashing and setting triangles

⅝ yard of pink print for binding

4½ yards of fabric for backing

69" x 77" piece of batting

## Cutting

From the white solid, cut:

11 strips, 2½" x 40"; crosscut into 86 rectangles, 2½" x 4½"

13 strips, 2½" x 40"

4 strips, 14" x 40"; crosscut into 7 squares, 14" x 14". Cut each square twice diagonally to yield 28 side setting triangles; 2 are extra.

1 strip, 8" x 40"; crosscut into 2 squares, 8" x 8". Cut each square once diagonally to yield 4 corner setting triangles.★

From the pink print, cut:

7 strips, 2¼" x 40"

★*Setting triangles are cut larger than needed and will extend beyond blocks.*

## Making the Blocks

**1.** Divide the 98 coordinating 5" squares into 49 pairs, combining two contrasting colors or contrasting values (light and dark).

**2.** Layer each pair of squares right sides together and, using ¼" seam allowance, stitch along two opposite sides of the squares as shown.

**3.** Cut down the center of the squares as shown and press the seam allowances open. Make a total of 98 two-patch units.

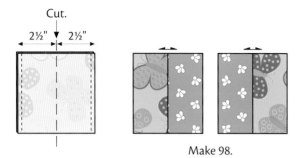

Make 98.

**4.** Divide the 98 two-patch units from step 3 into 49 new combinations of contrasting pairs.

**5.** With right sides together, layer the two-patch units, aligning the seams. Using ¼" seam allowance, stitch along two opposite sides making sure to stitch across the previous seam lines as shown.

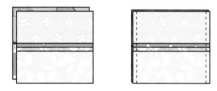

**6.** Cut down the center of the sewn units as shown and press the seam allowances open. Make a total of 98 Four Patch blocks. The blocks should measure 4½" x 4½".

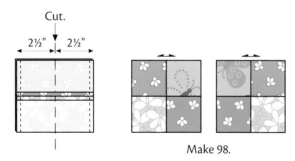

Make 98.

## Assembling the Quilt

**1.** Arrange and sew Four Patch blocks and white 2½" x 4½" sashing rectangles together into rows. Make two of each as shown. Each row begins and ends with a Four Patch block. Begin with a row of three Four Patch blocks, then five, seven, nine, eleven, and twelve.

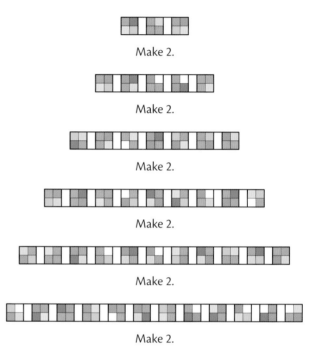

Make 2.

Make 2.

Make 2.

Make 2.

Make 2.

Make 2.

**2.** Sew the 13 white 2½" x 40" sashing strips together end to end.

**3.** From the pieced strip, cut the following lengths. Measure your rows first and make adjustments if needed.

- 2 strips, 2½" x 16½"
- 2 strips, 2½" x 28½"
- 2 strips, 2½" x 40½"
- 2 strips, 2½" x 52½"
- 2 strips, 2½" x 64½"
- 1 strip, 2½" x 70½"

**4.** Attach the corresponding sashing strip to each row as shown, except for the two longest rows (center rows) with 12 blocks each.

 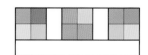

**5.** Sew the 2½" x 70½" sashing strip between the two center rows.

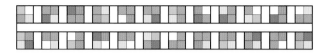

**6.** Arrange one Four Patch block, one white 2½" x 4½" sashing piece, and two white side setting triangles as shown. Sew and trim the triangles. Add the white corner triangle. Make four. The corner triangles will be trimmed later.

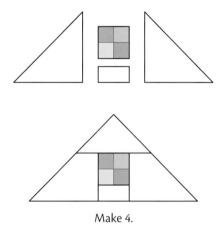

Make 4.

**7.** Lay out the rows, side setting triangles, and corner units in a diagonal setting on a design wall or flat surface. Sew the setting triangles to the ends of the rows. The triangles were cut oversized and the points will extend beyond the blocks.

**8.** Trim the setting triangles even with the top edge of each row.

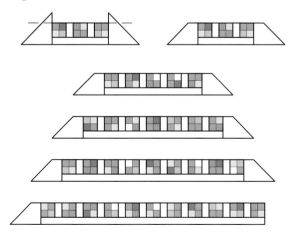

**9.** Referring to the assembly diagram, arrange and sew the rows together. Start with the center unit and work outward. Attach the corner units last.

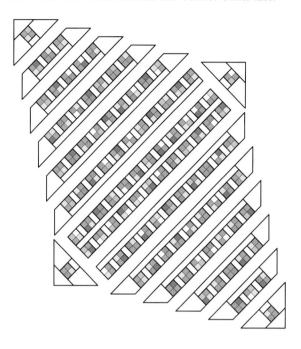

**10.** Trim the sides and square up the corners of the quilt as shown, cutting 2" beyond the points of the Four Patch blocks. The quilt should now measure 60½" x 69".

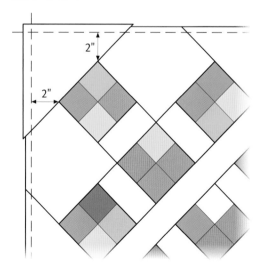

## Finishing

Refer to "Finishing" on page 75 to layer, baste, quilt, and add the binding using the pink print 2¼" x 40" strips.

# Four-Patch Pillowcase

Finished pillowcase: 20½" x 31" (for standard bed pillow)  •  Finished block: 4" x 4"

DESIGNED AND PIECED BY MARY JACOBSON AND BARBARA GROVES

This easy pillowcase coordinates with our Confetti quilt. We make pillowcases for every occasion, and they make great gift bags when giving a quilt as a gift. Barb's husband belongs to a Harley motorcycle group. For every trip they take, she makes the guys matching pillowcases from skull-and-crossbones fabrics she collects. When she first started this tradition, they made fun of it, but now they look forward to the pillowcase each time they ride off.

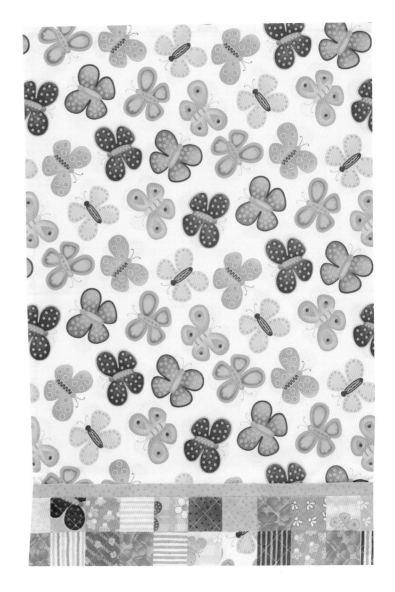

## Materials for One Pillowcase

*Note that the yardage for the pillowcase body must be at least 42" wide after prewashing and trimming the selvages off.*

22 coordinating 5" x 5" squares for blocks
1 yard of print fabric for pillowcase body
⅛ yard of print fabric for accent trim

## Cutting

See the Cutting Diagram below when cutting the print for the body.

From the print for the body, cut:
1 rectangle, 27½" x 42"

From the print for the accent trim, cut:
1 strip, 2" x 42"

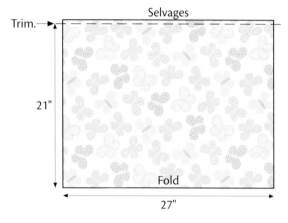

Cutting diagram

## Making the Blocks

**1.** Divide the 22 coordinating 5" squares into 11 pairs, combining two contrasting colors or values (light and dark).

**2.** Layer each pair of squares right sides together and, using ¼" seam allowance, stitch along two opposite sides of the squares as shown.

**3.** Cut down the center of the squares as shown and press the seam allowances open. Make a total of 22 two-patch units.

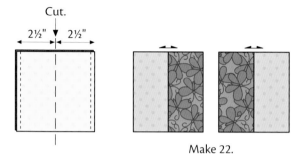

Make 22.

**4.** Divide the 22 two-patch units from step 3 into 11 *new* combinations of contrasting pairs.

**5.** With right sides together, layer the two-patch units, aligning the seams. Using ¼" seam allowance, stitch along two opposite sides making sure to stitch across the previous seam lines as shown.

**6.** Cut down the center of the sewn units as shown and press the seam allowances open. Make a total of 22 Four Patch blocks. The blocks should measure 4½" x 4½".

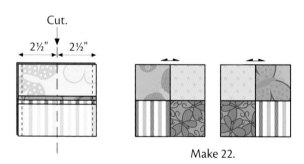

Make 22.

## Assembling the Pillowcase

**1.** Arrange and sew two rows of 11 Four Patch blocks each.

**2.** Sew the rows together to create a four-patch cuff as shown and trim to measure 8½" x 42".

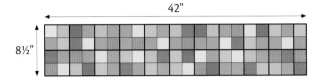

**3.** Lay the cuff strip *right side up* and lay the body fabric right side up on top of the cuff strip so that the top edges are even.

**4.** Press the accent strip in half *wrong sides together*. Lay the strip on top of the body fabric so that all raw edges are even.

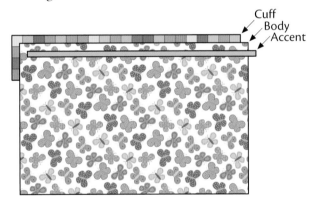

**5.** Use a few pins along the top edges to hold all of the layers together.

**6.** Beginning at the bottom, roll the body fabric up toward the top pinned edges.

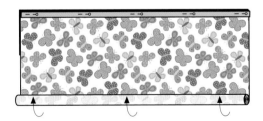

**7.** When you can see the bottom edge of the cuff (right side), gently pull the cuff over the rolled body fabric, aligning the raw edges with the previously pinned raw edges to create a tube. Pin well, making sure not to catch the rolled portion of the body fabric in the seam.

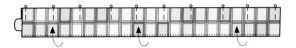

**8.** Using ¼" seam allowance, stitch along the top edge of the tube. You will be stitching through five layers: cuff, body, two edges of the accent fabric, and the other cuff edge.

**9.** Remove the pins and gently pull the body fabric out of the tube. Press the accent strip away from the cuff.

**10.** If desired, sew a quilting design in the four-patch cuff area to add texture and stability.

**11.** Fold the pillowcase wrong sides together. Make sure to match the cuff and accent pieces along the side. Pin as needed. Using a scant ¼" seam allowance, sew down the side, and then across the bottom of the case. Remember you are sewing on the right side of the fabric!

**12.** Turn the pillowcase wrong side out and press.

**13.** Sew, using a ⅜" seam allowance, down the side of the pillowcase and then again across the bottom of the case being sure to not catch the previous seam allowances. Remember this time you are sewing on the *wrong side* of the fabric!

**14.** Turn the pillowcase right side out and press.

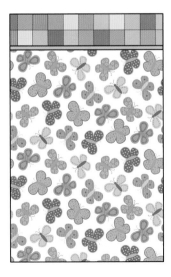

# BFF

Finished quilt: 64" x 80"  •  Finished block: 8" x 8"

DESIGNED AND PIECED BY BARBARA GROVES AND MARY JACOBSON

BFF–Best Friends Forever! We love Pinwheel and Four Patch blocks, and the combination turned out fabulous in this whimsical quilt. Using black is a first for us–we generally keep far away from black, but this border fabric had so many appealing colors in it we couldn't resist. Make this fun quilt with your BFF!

## Materials

*All yardages are based on 40"-wide fabric.*

96 coordinating 5" x 5" squares for blocks

2⅜ yards of black print for Pinwheel blocks and outer border

1 yard of white-with-red-dot fabric for Pinwheel blocks

1 yard of black-with-white-dot fabric for inner border and binding

5¼ yards of fabric for backing

72" x 88" piece of batting

## Cutting

From the white-with-red-dot fabric, cut:

6 strips, 4⅞" x 40"; crosscut into 48 squares, 4⅞" x 4⅞"

From the black print, cut:

6 strips, 4⅞" x 40"; crosscut into 48 squares, 4⅞" x 4⅞"

7 strips, 6¾" x 40"

From the black-with-white-dot fabric, cut:

6 strips, 2" x 40"

8 strips, 2¼" x 40"

## Making the Pinwheel Blocks

**1.** Draw a diagonal line on the wrong side of each white-with-red-dot 4⅞" square.

**2.** Layer one white-with-red-dot and one black print 4⅞" square right sides together with the white-with-red-dot square on top. Stitch ¼" from each side of the drawn line, cut apart on the drawn line, and press. The half-square-triangle units should measure 4½" x 4½". Make 96.

Make 96.

**3.** Arrange and sew four half-square-triangle units into a Pinwheel block as shown. Make 24 Pinwheel blocks. The blocks should measure 8½" x 8½".

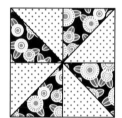

Make 24.

## Making the Four Patch Blocks

**1.** Divide the 96 coordinating 5" squares into 48 pairs, combining two contrasting colors or contrasting values (light and dark).

**2.** Layer each pair of squares right sides together, and using ¼" seam allowance, stitch along two opposite sides of the squares as shown.

**3.** Cut down the center of the squares as shown and press the seam allowances open. Make a total of 96 two-patch units.

Cut.

2½"    2½"

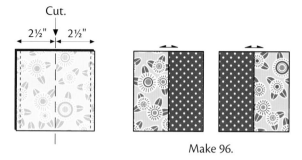

Make 96.

**4.** Divide the 96 two-patch units from step 3 into 48 new combinations of contrasting pairs.

**5.** With right sides together, layer the two-patch units, aligning the seams. Using ¼" seam allowance, stitch along two opposite sides, making sure to stitch across the previous seam lines as shown.

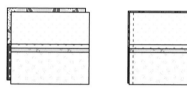

**6.** Cut down the center of the sewn units as shown and press the seam allowances open. Make a total of 96 Four Patch blocks.

Cut.

2½"    2½"

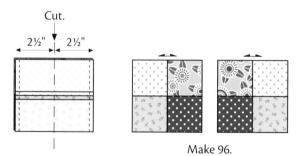

Make 96.

**7.** Arrange and sew four of the Four Patch blocks together into Sixteen Patch blocks as shown. The Sixteen Patch blocks should measure 8½" x 8½". Make 24 Sixteen Patch blocks.

Make 24.

## Assembling the Quilt

**1.** Referring to the quilt diagram, arrange the blocks in eight rows of six blocks each, alternating them as shown. Sew the blocks into rows.

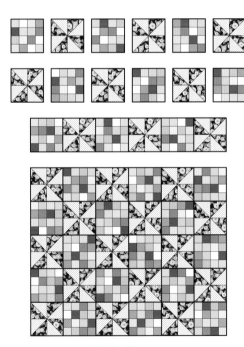

Quilt diagram

**2.** Sew the rows together. The quilt should now measure 48½" x 64½".

## Adding the Borders

**1.** Piece six black-with-white-dot 2" x 40" inner-border strips together end to end.

**2.** Measure the quilt from top to bottom through the middle to determine the length of the side borders.

**3.** From the pieced strip, cut the side borders to the needed length and attach them to the sides of the quilt.

**4.** Measure the quilt from side to side through the middle including the side borders to determine the length of the top and bottom borders.

**5.** From the pieced strip, cut the top and bottom borders to the needed length and attach them to the top and bottom of the quilt. The quilt should now measure 51½" x 67½".

**6.** Piece the seven black print 6¾" x 40" outer-border strips end to end.

**7.** Repeat the measuring and cutting process as you did for the inner borders. Add the black print outer borders. The quilt should now measure 64" x 80".

## Finishing

Refer to "Finishing" on page 75 to layer, baste, quilt, and add the binding using the black-with-white-dot 2¼" x 40" strips.

# Rebecca

Finished quilt: 71" x 85"  •  Finished block: 9" x 9"

DESIGNED AND PIECED BY MARY JACOBSON AND BARBARA GROVES

This quilt is named after our niece Rebecca. For years, our sister Terry has been leaving not-so-subtle hints that we should name a quilt after her daughter. We named one of our first patterns after her daughter Sarah, and we have been reminded of the neglected Rebecca ever since. Hope we don't have to start naming quilts after her grandchildren and cats!

## Materials

*All yardages are based on 40"-wide fabric.*

50 coordinating 10" x 10" squares for blocks

2¼ yards of pink print for first and third borders and binding

2 yards of white solid for blocks, sashing, and second border

5½ yards of fabric for backing

79" x 93" piece of batting

## Cutting

From the white solid, cut:

4 strips, 2½" x 40"; crosscut into 64 squares, 2½" x 2½"

10 strips, 1½" x 40"; crosscut into 38 rectangles, 1½" x 9½"

23 strips, 1½" x 40"

From the pink print, cut:

15 strips, 3½" x 40"

9 strips, 2¼" x 40"

## Making the Four Patch Flip Blocks

Choose thirty-two of the fifty 10" squares for the flip blocks. The remaining 18 will be used for the setting blocks on the sides and corners.

**1.** Draw a diagonal line on the wrong side of the white 2½" squares.

**2.** Select sixteen of the thirty-two 10" squares. Place one white 2½" square on each corner. Stitch on the drawn lines. Trim the seam allowance to ¼", flip, and press. Make 16.

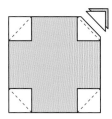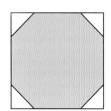

Make 16.

**3.** Layer one block from step 2 and one 10" square right sides together. Using ¼" seam allowance, stitch along two opposite sides of the squares as shown.

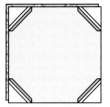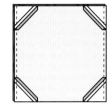

**4.** Cut down the center of the squares as shown and press the seam allowances open. Make 32 units.

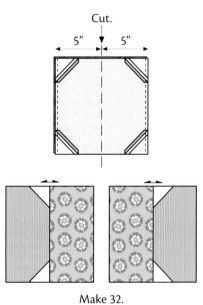

Make 32.

**5.** Divide the 32 units from step 4 into 16 *new* pairs of contrasting colors or values.

**6.** With right sides together, layer the units, aligning the seams. Make sure that the white corners are opposite each other as shown. Using ¼" seam allowance, stitch along two opposite sides, making sure to stitch across the previous seam lines as shown.

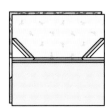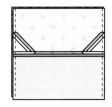

**7.** Cut down the center of the sewn units as shown and press the seam allowances open. The blocks should now measure 9½" x 9½". Make a total of 32 Four Patch Flip blocks.

Make 32.

## Making Blocks for Setting Triangles

**1.** Divide the 18 coordinating 10" squares into 9 pairs, combining two contrasting colors or contrasting values (light and dark).

**2.** Layer each pair of squares right sides together, and, using ¼" seam allowance, stitch along two opposite sides of the squares as shown.

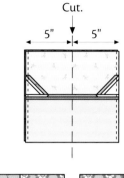

**3.** Cut down the center of the squares as shown and press the seam allowances open. Make a total of 18 two-patch units.

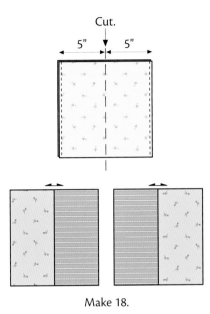

Make 18.

**4.** Divide the 18 two-patch units from step 3 into 9 *new* combinations of contrasting pairs.

**5.** With right sides together, layer the two-patch units, aligning the seams. Using ¼" seam allowance, stitch along two opposite sides making sure to stitch across the previous seam lines as shown.

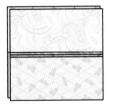

**6.** Cut down the center of the sewn units as shown and press the seam allowances open. Make a total of 18 Four Patch blocks. The blocks should

measure 9½" x 9½". These blocks will be cut later for the side and corner setting blocks. Adding some spray starch when pressing will give them extra stability.

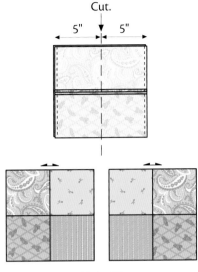

Make 18.

**7.** Cut only *four* blocks in half diagonally as shown, adding ¼" for seam allowances. Align the ¼" line of your ruler with opposite corners of the block. These will be the corner setting triangles; the cut-off pieces will not be used.

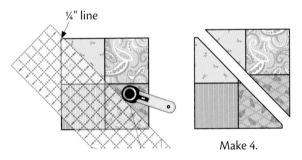

Make 4.

## Assembling the Quilt

**1.** Sew 15 of the white 1½" x 40" strips together end to end for the sashing.

**2.** From the pieced strip, cut:
- 2 strips, 1½" x 29½"
- 2 strips, 1½" x 31½"
- 2 strips, 1½" x 49½"
- 2 strips, 1½" x 69½"
- 3 strips, 1½" x 79½"

**3.** Referring to the assembly diagram, arrange the blocks and sashing strips into diagonal rows. The side setting blocks will be trimmed later. Sew the blocks and 1½" x 9½" sashing strips into rows.

**4.** Working from the center outward, sew the block rows and sashing strips together. Add the corner blocks last, aligning the center seam with the center seam of the Four Patch Flip block in the adjacent rows.

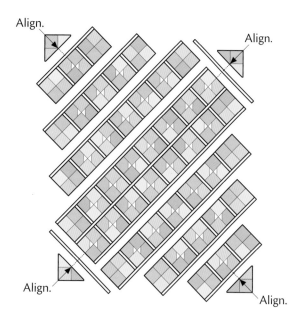

**5.** Trim the sides and square up the corners of the quilt as shown, cutting ¼" from the center points of the side setting blocks.

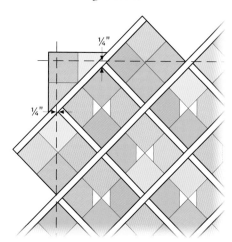

## Adding the Borders

**1.** Piece seven of the pink print 3½" x 40" strips together end to end for the first border.

**2.** Measure the quilt from top to bottom through the middle to determine the length of the side borders.

**3.** From the pieced strip, cut side borders to the needed length and attach them to the sides of the quilt.

**4.** Measure the quilt from side to side through the middle including the side borders to determine the length of the top and bottom borders.

**5.** From the pieced strip, cut the top and bottom borders to the needed length and attach them to the quilt. Sew carefully, as the edges of the quilt will be bias. Using a walking foot will help feed the layers evenly.

**6.** Piece eight white 1½" x 40" strips together end to end for the second border.

**7.** Repeat the measuring and cutting process as you did for the first border to add the white borders to your quilt.

**8.** Piece eight pink print 3½" x 40" strips together end to end for the third border.

**9.** Repeat the measuring and cutting process and add the outer pink borders to the quilt.

## Finishing

Refer to "Finishing" on page 75 to layer, baste, quilt, and add the binding using the pink print 2¼" x 40" strips.

# Swatches

Finished quilt: 82" x 90" • Finished blocks: 8" x 8"

DESIGNED AND PIECED BY BARBARA GROVES AND MARY JACOBSON

Our take on a Square in a Square block turns out to be a Four Patch in a Square block. Making this quilt is a perfect way to use all those fun precut 5" and 10" squares you've been seeing in all the quilt shops! Our quilt goes together quickly with an added bonus of looking like it's on point, but without all the pesky setting triangles. We had a blast making this quilt! Hope you enjoy it too!

## Materials

*All yardages are based on 40"-wide fabric.*
90 coordinating 5" x 5" squares for blocks
90 coordinating 10" x 10" squares for blocks
1½ yards of blue floral for border
¾ yard of blue print for binding
8½ yards of fabric for backing
90" x 98" piece of batting

## Cutting

From the 10" x 10" squares, cut:
Each square twice diagonally to yield 360
　triangles★

From the blue floral, cut:
9 strips, 5¼" x 40"

From the blue print, cut:
9 strips, 2¼" x 40"

*★The triangles are larger than needed and will be trimmed later. Keep like triangles together.*

## Making the Blocks

**1.** Divide the 90 coordinating 5" squares into 45 pairs, combining two contrasting colors or contrasting values (light and dark).

**2.** Layer each pair of squares with right sides together, and using ¼" seam allowance, stitch along two opposite sides of the squares as shown.

**3.** Cut down the center of the squares as shown and press the seam allowances open. Make a total of 90 two-patch units.

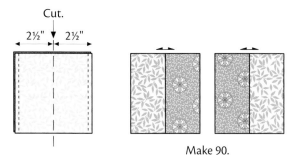

Make 90.

**4.** Divide the 90 two-patch units from step 3 into 45 *new* combinations of contrasting pairs.

**5.** With right sides together, layer the two-patch units together, aligning the seams. Using ¼" seam allowance, stitch along two opposite sides, making sure to stitch across the previous seam lines as shown.

**6.** Cut down the center of the sewn units as shown and press the seam allowances open. Make 90 Four Patch blocks.

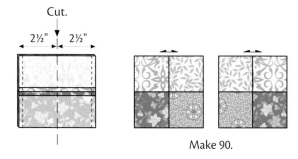

Make 90.

**7.** Select one Four Patch block and four matching triangles to make the Four Patch in a Square block. Crease the triangles in the center and align them with the center seam of the Four Patch block. Sew the triangles to opposite sides of the Four Patch block. Trim the triangles even with

the Four Patch block. Add the remaining two triangles. Press the blocks using a little spray starch to add stability.

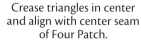

Crease triangles in center and align with center seam of Four Patch.

Trim triangles even with Four Patch.

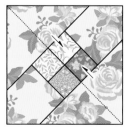

Crease triangles in center and align with center seam of Four Patch.

**8.** Trim the block to measure 8½" x 8½". Make 90 Four Patch in a Square blocks.

## Assembling the Quilt

**1.** Referring to the quilt diagram, arrange the blocks into 10 rows of nine blocks each. Sew the blocks into rows and sew the rows together. The quilt should now measure 72½" x 80½".

**2.** Piece the nine blue floral 5¼" x 40" border strips together end to end.

**3.** Measure the quilt from top to bottom through the middle to determine the length of the side borders.

**4.** From the pieced strip, cut the side borders to the needed length and attach them to the sides of the quilt.

**5.** Measure the quilt from side to side through the middle including the side borders to determine the length of the top and bottom borders.

**6.** From the pieced strip, cut the top and bottom borders to the needed length and attach them to the quilt.

## Finishing

Refer to "Finishing" on page 75 to layer, baste, quilt, and add the binding using the blue print 2¼" x 40" strips.

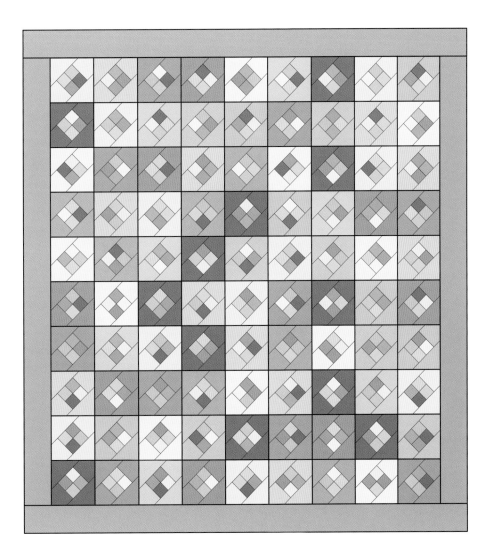

# S-C-H-Double-Oh-L

Finished quilt: 80" x 80"  •  Finished block: 8" x 8"

DESIGNED AND PIECED BY BARBARA GROVES AND MARY JACOBSON

Spells school!! Remember this fun jump-rope jingle from your grade school days? The navy blue chain running through this quilt reminds us of twirling jump ropes. Remember double Dutch and "Don't Forget the Red Hot Peppers"? We used old school and feedsack reproduction prints to make this nostalgic quilt. Dick and Jane would just love it!

## Materials

*All yardages are based on 40"-wide fabric.*

24 coordinating fat quarters for blocks

2 yards of dark blue print for blocks and inner border

1⅝ yards of green print for outer border

⅔ yard of orange print for binding

7½ yards of fabric for backing

88" x 88" piece of batting

## Cutting

**From each fat quarter, cut:**

1 strip, 5" x 20" (24 total); crosscut the strips into a total of 64 squares, 5" x 5"

2 strips, 4½" x 20" (48 total); crosscut the strips into a total of 144 squares, 4½" x 4½"★

**From the dark blue print, cut:**

8 strips, 5" x 40"; crosscut into 64 squares, 5" x 5"

7 strips, 2½" x 40"

**From the green print, cut:**

8 strips, 6¼" x 40"

**From the orange print, cut:**

9 strips, 2¼" x 40"

★*Keep like prints together in pairs.*

## Making the Blocks

**1.** Layer one coordinating print 5" square and one dark blue 5" square right sides together. Using ¼" seam allowance, stitch along two opposite sides of the squares as shown.

**2.** Cut down the center of the squares as shown and press the seam allowances open. Make a total of 128 two-patch units.

Cut.

2½"    2½"

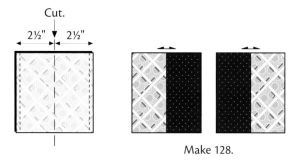

Make 128.

**3.** With right sides together, layer the two-patch units, aligning the seams and reversing the color placement as shown. Using ¼" seam allowance, stitch along two opposite sides making sure to stitch across the previous seam lines.

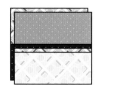

**4.** Cut down the center of the sewn units as shown and press the seam allowances open. Make 128 Four Patch blocks.

Cut.

2½"    2½"

Make 128.

**5.** For each Double Four Patch block, choose two matching Four Patch blocks and two matching 4½" squares; the print should be different from the ones used in the Four Patch blocks. You will

have extra 4½" squares, so choose your favorites. Arrange and sew the blocks as shown. The blocks should measure 8½" x 8½". Make 64 Double Four Patch blocks.

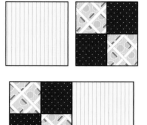

Make 64.

## Assembling the Quilt

**1.** Arrange the blocks into eight rows of eight blocks each, rotating the blocks as shown. Sew the blocks into rows.

Make 4.

Make 4.

**2.** Sew the rows together. The quilt should now measure 64½" x 64½".

## Adding the Borders

**1.** Piece the seven dark blue 2½" x 40" strips together end to end for the inner border.

**2.** Measure the quilt from top to bottom through the middle to determine the length of the side borders.

**3.** From the pieced strip, cut the side borders to the needed length and attach them to the sides of the quilt.

**4.** Measure the quilt from side to side through the middle including the side borders to determine the length of the top and bottom borders.

**5.** From the pieced strip, cut the top and bottom borders to the needed length and attach them to the quilt. The quilt should now measure 68½" x 68½".

**6.** Piece the eight green print 6¼" x 40" strips together end to end for the outer border.

**7.** Repeat the measuring and cutting process as you did for the inner border and add the outer border to the quilt. The quilt should now measure 80" x 80".

## Finishing

Refer to "Finishing" on page 75 to layer, baste, quilt, and add the binding using the orange print 2¼" x 40" strips.

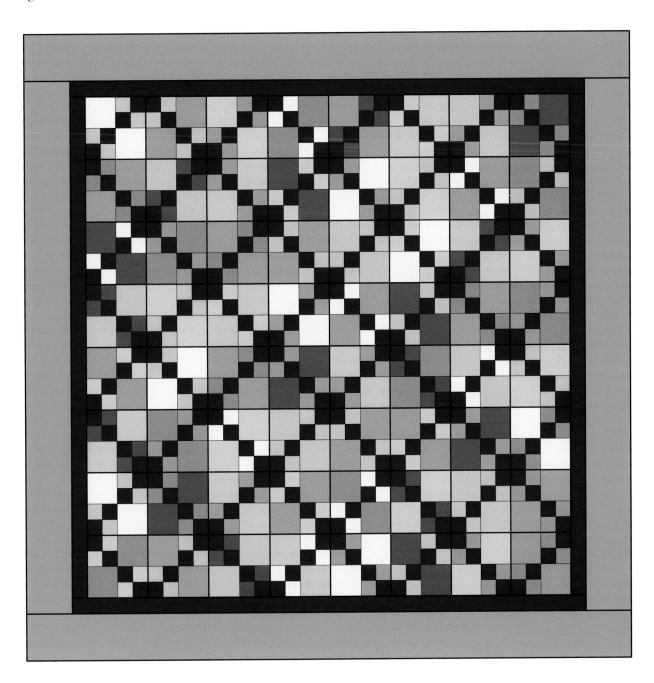

# General Instructions

These general instructions are to help you along your quilting way, but feel free to use your own tried-and-true methods. Enjoy!

## Fabric

All the quilts in this book are made from high-quality 100%-cotton fabrics, and the yardages are based on 40"-wide fabrics. We encourage you to buy extra yardage to allow for shrinkage, trimming selvages, fixing errors—or a slipped ruler.

Prewash, tumble dry, and press the fabrics before using them. We don't like any surprises after we have worked so hard on our quilts, so we strongly recommend that you launder the fabrics the same way you would the completed quilt.

## Cutting

All cutting instructions for the projects in this book include a ¼" seam allowance.

Rotary tools have made cutting fast and accurate. Basic tools are a self-healing cutting mat, a rotary cutter, and clear acrylic rulers with easy-to-read measurements.

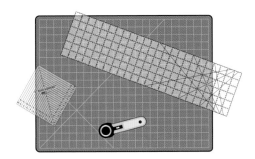

Before cutting, fold and press all fabrics in half, matching the selvages. Place the folded edge closest to you on the cutting mat. When cutting strips, always start with a straightened edge. Align a square ruler along the folded edge of the fabric. Place a longer ruler to the left of the square ruler, just covering the uneven raw edges.

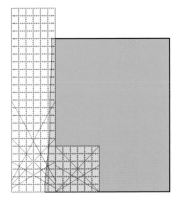

Remove the square ruler and cut along the right edge of the long ruler.

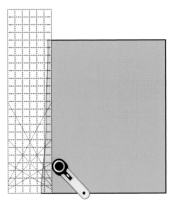

Place the long ruler on the fabric so that the ruler marking of the desired width is aligned with the cut edge of the fabric. Cut from the fold to the selvages; stop every few strips and square up the edge of the fabric again to avoid a curve in the strips.

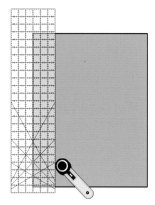

Cutting on the crosswise grain refers to cutting from the fold of the fabric to the selvages. This means cutting from selvage to selvage. The crosswise grain has slightly more give and stretch than the lengthwise grain of the fabric.

Cutting on the lengthwise grain refers to cutting parallel to the selvage edge. Lengthwise grain has the least amount of stretch or give.

## Machine Piecing

It "seams" the most important thing to remember in machine piecing is to maintain an accurate ¼" seam allowance. This will keep all your quilt blocks the desired finished size, and the pieces will fit together perfectly. Set your machine stitch length to 10 to 12 stitches per inch for a strong seam.

## Pressing

The traditional rule in quiltmaking is to press seam allowances to one side, toward the darker color when possible. We, however, like to press our seam allowances open to reduce bulk at seam intersections and give us more accuracy.

## Measuring and Adding Borders

After you have sewn all the blocks and rows together, it's time to add the borders. The instructions for each quilt give you the width and number of border strips to piece together.

Measure the quilt from top to bottom through the middle to determine the length of the side borders. Measure the quilt through the center to determine border lengths. This will provide a more accurate measurement, as some stretching and waving of the outer edges may have occurred during construction. From the pieced border strips, cut the side borders to the measured length. Mark the centers of the border strips and the quilt top. Pin the borders to the sides of the quilt at the center and ends. Sew the side borders; some easing may be required.

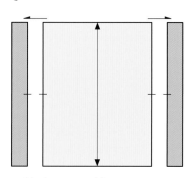

Mark centers. Measure center of quilt, top to bottom.

Measure the quilt from side to side through the middle, including the just-added side borders, to determine the length of the top and bottom borders. From the pieced border strips, cut the top and bottom borders to the measured length. Mark the centers of the border strips and the quilt top. Pin the borders to the top and bottom of the quilt at the center and ends. Sew the top and bottom borders; some easing may be required.

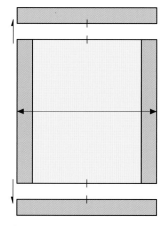

Mark centers. Measure center of quilt, side to side, including borders.

# Finishing

Once the quilt top is complete, the next step is to actually make it into a quilt. The backing and batting are layered with the top and all three layers are basted together. Once that is done, the quilting, binding, and any finishing touches are added.

### LAYERING THE QUILT

We recommend cutting the quilt backing and batting 4" larger than the quilt top on all sides. It might be necessary to piece the backing of your quilt using two or three lengths of fabric. We prefer to use a vertical seam on all of our quilts, and the yardages in the materials lists reflect that. Sometimes leftover fabrics and blocks from the quilt top have found their way into our pieced backings, and that has given us those few extra inches needed to avoid a second or third length of backing fabric.

Spread the backing wrong side up on a flat surface. To keep the backing from moving, use masking tape at the corners and sides to hold it in place. Place the batting over the backing and smooth out any wrinkles. Center the pressed quilt top right side up on top of the batting, once again smoothing out any wrinkles.

### BASTING

Use rustproof safety pins for basting the layers together, starting from the center and working your way to the sides. Place the pins 3" to 4" apart, smoothing as you go. Some quiltmakers prefer to use thread to baste the layers together, particularly for hand quilting. If you choose to use thread, use white sewing thread and make large basting stitches about 2" to 3" apart.

### QUILTING

Hand or machine quilt as desired. Our desire is that someone else quilt our projects! (We love Darlene, our long-arm machine quilter.) After the quilting is complete, trim the excess batting and backing even with the quilt top.

### STRAIGHT-GRAIN BINDING

Binding finishes the raw edges of your quilt. Use straight-grain binding when the edges of the quilt are straight. Each of the quilt projects in this book will give you the required number of binding strips needed as well as the binding method to use.

**1.** With right sides together, join the ends of the strips on the diagonal to create one long binding strip. Trim the seam allowances to ¼" and press the seam allowances open.

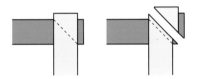

**2.** Fold the binding strip in half lengthwise with wrong sides together and press.

**3.** Position the binding on the front of the quilt with raw edges aligned. We recommend starting at the center of one of the sides and leaving a 10" tail (for joining the ends) before beginning the stitching. Using a ¼" seam allowance and a walking foot, sew the binding to the side of the quilt, stopping ¼" from the corner; carefully backstitch 3 or 4 stitches. Clip the thread and remove the quilt from the sewing machine.

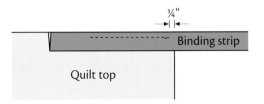

**4.** Fold the binding strip up, so the fold creates a 45° angle.

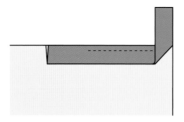

**5.** Holding the 45° fold in place, bring the binding back down onto itself and fold it even with the quilt edge. Begin stitching at the folded edge through all layers; carefully backstitch. Continue stitching to the next corner and around the quilt in the same manner.

**6.** When you have reached a point approximately 10" from the starting point, stop and remove the quilt from the sewing machine.

**7.** To join the binding ends, fold both strips back along the edge of the quilt so that the folded edges meet an equal distance from both lines of stitching. Press to crease the folds.

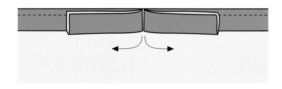

**8.** Cut both strips 1⅛" from the folds. Open both strips and place the ends at a right angle to each other, right sides together. Join the strips with a diagonal seam as shown. Trim the seam allowance to ¼" and press open.

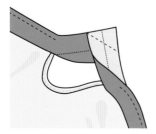

**9.** Fold the joined strips so that the wrong sides are together again and place the binding flat against the quilt. Finish stitching across the edge of the quilt.

**10.** Turn the binding over to the back of the quilt and hand stitch using a blind stitch. Make sure to cover the machine stitching. Miter each corner by folding down one side first and then the other.

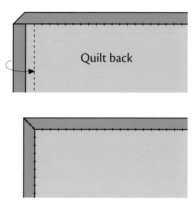

Quilt back

## MITERING 135° CORNERS

**1.** Mark the pivot point where the ¼" seam lines will intersect at the 135° corner of the quilt with a pin.

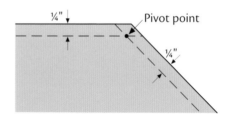

¼"   Pivot point   ¼"

**2.** Position the binding on the front of the quilt with raw edges aligned.

**3.** Sew the binding to the side of the quilt, stopping at the pivot point; carefully backstitch 3 to 4 stitches. Clip the thread and remove the quilt from the sewing machine.

**4.** Fold the binding strip up, so the fold creates a 45° angle.

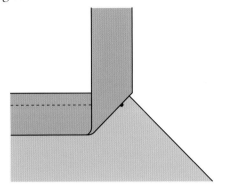

**5.** Fold the binding down onto itself and align the raw edges of the binding along the edge of the quilt, following the 135° angle of the corner. Start stitching again at the pivot point. Backstitch off the quilt and then stitch forward continuing the ¼" seam allowance.

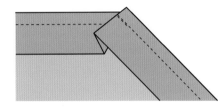

## BIAS BINDING

Bias binding is used when the quilt has curved edges. Cutting the strips along the bias gives the fabric the stretch it needs to lie flat along the curved edge.

**1.** Cut the bias binding fabric into a square according to the project directions. On the wrong side, mark the top and bottom with a pin, and cut the square in half on the diagonal.

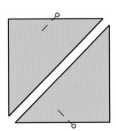

**2.** Using a ¼" seam allowance, sew the two triangles, right sides together, along the marked edges. Press the seam allowances open.

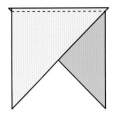

**3.** On the wrong side, mark parallel lines 2¼" apart.

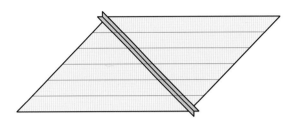

**4.** With right sides together, and offsetting the marked lines by one width, sew the fabric into a tube using a ¼" seam allowance.

**5.** Press the seam allowances open and cut along the marked lines to make one continuous strip of bias binding.

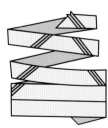

**6.** Continue with steps 2–10 of "Straight-Grain Binding" on page 75 to press and attach the binding to the quilt.

# About the Authors

Barb and Mary both live in Phoenix, Arizona, with their families—cats and dogs included. Their belief in fast, fun, and easy designs can be seen in the quilts created for their pattern company, in their many books, and in their fabric designs for Moda.

These fun-loving sisters have their hands in all aspects of quilting. When not teaching or designing new fabrics and patterns, they have found the time to make everyone's sewing projects easier. They are the creative minds behind the ever-popular SideWinder™, the portable bobbin winder by Wrights.

To see what these two are currently up to, visit their website at meandmysisterdesigns.com.

# New Best-Selling Titles from

America's Best-Loved Quilt Books®

America's Best-Loved Craft & Hobby Books®
America's Best-Loved Knitting Books®

## APPLIQUÉ
Appliqué Quilt Revival
Beautiful Blooms
Cutting-Garden Quilts
Dream Landscapes
**Easy Appliqué Blocks**—*NEW!*
**Simple Comforts**—*NEW!*
Sunbonnet Sue and Scottie Too

## BABIES AND CHILDREN
Baby's First Quilts
Baby Wraps
Let's Pretend
The Little Box of Baby Quilts
Snuggle-and-Learn Quilts for Kids
Sweet and Simple Baby Quilts

## BEGINNER
Color for the Terrified Quilter
Happy Endings, Revised Edition
Machine Appliqué for the Terrified Quilter
Your First Quilt Book (or it should be!)

## GENERAL QUILTMAKING
Adventures in Circles
American Jane's Quilts for All Seasons
Bits and Pieces
**Bold and Beautiful**—*NEW!*
Cool Girls Quilt
Country-Fresh Quilts
Creating Your Perfect Quilting Space
**Fig Tree Quilts: Fresh Vintage Sewing**—
*NEW!*
**Folk-Art Favorites**—*NEW!*
Follow-the-Line Quilting Designs
Volume Three
Gathered from the Garden
The New Handmade
Points of View
Prairie Children and Their Quilts
Quilt Revival
A Quilter's Diary
Quilter's Happy Hour
Quilting for Joy
**Remembering Adelia**—*NEW!*
Sensational Sashiko

Simple Seasons
Skinny Quilts and Table Runners
**That Patchwork Place® Quilt Collection—**
*NEW!*
Twice Quilted
Young at Heart Quilts

## HOLIDAY AND SEASONAL
Christmas Quilts from Hopscotch
Comfort and Joy
Holiday Wrappings

## HOOKED RUGS, NEEDLE FELTING, AND PUNCHNEEDLE
The Americana Collection
Miniature Punchneedle Embroidery
Needle-Felting Magic
Needle Felting with Cotton and Wool

## PAPER PIECING
Easy Reversible Vests, Revised Edition
Paper-Pieced Mini Quilts
Show Me How to Paper Piece
Showstopping Quilts to Foundation Piece
A Year of Paper Piecing

## PIECING
501 Rotary-Cut Quilt Blocks
Favorite Traditional Quilts Made Easy
Loose Change
Maple Leaf Quilts
Mosaic Picture Quilts
New Cuts for New Quilts
Nine by Nine
On-Point Quilts
Quiltastic Curves
Ribbon Star Quilts
Rolling Along

## QUICK QUILTS
40 Fabulous Quick-Cut Quilts
Instant Bargello
Quilts on the Double
Sew Fun, Sew Colorful Quilts
**Supersize 'Em!**—*NEW!*

## SCRAP QUILTS
Nickel Quilts
Save the Scraps
**Scrap-Basket Surprises**—*NEW!*
Simple Strategies for Scrap Quilts
Spotlight on Scraps

## CRAFTS
**A to Z of Sewing**—*NEW!*
Art from the Heart
The Beader's Handbook
Card Design
Crochet for Beaders
Dolly Mama Beads
Embellished Memories
Friendship Bracelets All Grown Up
Making Beautiful Jewelry
Paper It!
Trading Card Treasures

## KNITTING & CROCHET
365 Crochet Stitches a Year:
Perpetual Calendar
365 Knitting Stitches a Year:
Perpetual Calendar
A to Z of Knitting
All about Knitting
Amigurumi World
Beyond Wool
Cable Confidence
Casual, Elegant Knits
Crocheted Pursenalities
Gigi Knits…and Purls
Kitty Knits
Knitted Finger Puppets
The Knitter's Book of Finishing
Techniques
Knitting Circles around Socks
Knitting with Gigi
More Sensational Knitted Socks
Pursenalities
**Simple Stitches**—*NEW!*
Toe-Up Techniques for Hand Knit
Socks, Revised Edition
Together or Separate

1/09